Persistence of Vision

poems by

Donna Isaac

Finishing Line Press
Georgetown, Kentucky

Persistence of Vision

Copyright © 2019 by Donna Isaac
ISBN 978-1-64662-068-5 First Edition
All rights reserved under International and Pan-American Copyright Conventions. No part of this book may be reproduced in any manner whatsoever without written permission from the publisher, except in the case of brief quotations embodied in critical articles and reviews.

ACKNOWLEDGMENTS

"Holding On" appears in *Endlessly Rocking* under the title "The Good Girl."
A version of "grief" was published by *Clockhouse*, Vol. 7, Goddard College.

Publisher: Leah Maines
Editor: Christen Kincaid
Cover Art: Photo of the Paramount Theater in Charlottesville, Virginia by Laura Bittle <www.facebook.com/TheFickleArtist>
Author Photo: Donna Isaac
Cover Design: Elizabeth Maines McCleavy

Printed in the USA on acid-free paper.
Order online: www.finishinglinepress.com
       also available on amazon.com

       Author inquiries and mail orders:
            Finishing Line Press
              P. O. Box 1626
       Georgetown, Kentucky 40324
                U. S. A.

Table of Contents

Sallie Gardner 1
Cinephiles 2
kiddie matiness 3
Silver Screen Temple 4
For the Love of the Dance 6
Beatle Mania 7
Ruminations 8
Seeking 10
That's Entertainment 11
Hepburn 12
Bedford Falls 13
Conflict 14
Flight 15
Visualization 16
Parallels 17
Fear and Loathing 18
Ulysses as Porn 19
And the Winner Is 20
Something 21
Songcatcher 24
In the Midst of Movies, Poetry 25
Holding On 26
Ode to Hayley Mills 27
What She Wore Oscar Night, 2001 28
The Gunderson Baby 29
Sound Surround 30
Little Girl 31
grief 32
Patsey 33
Acting the Part 34
Notes and Movie Allusion Titles 35

Sallie Gardner

                           First

                           image

                            in

                           motion

sometimes all four legs off the ground of Palo Alto tail flashing mane flying
         Muybridge   with white
           piston- and   sheets
           like   Stanford   and
            legs   in   is   a trip
            like   awe   coming   wire
clockwork   at the image   clear   at
  back   foreleg   by   every
   and   fetlock   god a   turn
  forth   kick   galloping   the
   and   thrust   horse   picture

Cinephiles

In the dark of the theater,
a chomping, like horses.
I gnaw on cherry Nibs
counteracting the ambient crunch.

My mother liked Wallaby
gourmet black licorice,
risking hypertension.
She'd pick out the black
Jujyfruits, buy Twizzlers
or boxes of Good 'n Plenty.

In *The Gold Rush*,
the Little Tramp ingests
a whole shoe made of licorice.

Brilliant, bereft Charlie,
his dad, an alcoholic;
his mum, syphilitic, mad;
hounded by McCarthy, the press;
beloved by the Nazis
until they thought he was a Jew.
(Hitler was a fan,
shaving off his handlebar
for the Tramp's toothbrush.)

Charlie liked Lolitas,
perfectionism, the eyes
of orphans and flower girls.
We like prat-falling in the rain,
dangling from industrial cogs,
and toddling off into the sunset,
more adventures ahead
to chew on, to consume.

kiddie matinees

in movie theaters with royal names
with red velvet curtains and golden columns
we paid with bottle caps or coins
to see viking marauders bury
victims up to their necks
and release vipers to coil
about them on the sand
or to watch with doe-eyes
a warrior dressed in furry pelts
shove a half-naked blonde
down ravishing her in a tent
all this on the big screen
while we licked all-day suckers
green apple and cherry
or ruined our teeth with mary janes
or slo-pokes or laffy taffy
our mother never knew
about the violence the mayhem
showing at the saturday matinee
but just wanted us out of the house
so she could pine-sol the tile
or wax and buff the hardwood
with rented stiff-brushed machines
that spun and scrubbed off the dirt
and the scratches we dragged back
into the house after our day away
before we dreamt of long knives
and horned helmets on bearded men
who rode icy seas and slit throats
in the afternoon in the paramount theater

Silver Screen Temple

Shirley is a darlin',
all dimples and shiny curls.
She is movie-going magic,
a shiny star of a girl.

In *Baby Take a Bow*
in pink tutu she dances.
Audiences love tiny Shirley
as she simpers, pouts, and prances.

"On the Good Ship Lollipop"
a *Bright Eyes*' zippity tune;
"Animal Crackers in My Soup"
Curly Top to the orphans crooned.

As the littlest beribboned rebel,
in pantalets and Confederate cap,
with Bojangles on the stairs,
a pas de deux in tap.

A dance with Buddy Ebsen
in pants and middy blouse,
cutting a rug "At the Codfish Ball,"
Shirley brought down the house.

Heidi in the snowy Swiss Alps
loves Baerli and goatherd Peter.
She needs her gruff old Grandfather
to love her and complete her.

A favorite role as Sarah Crewe,
her father, killed in the Boer War,
the princess, now a lowly servant,
forced to do every menial chore.

Until one day Ram Dass blesses her
with blankets, food, and fire.
She finds her father recuperating,
circumstances no longer dire.

The Blue Bird and later films
essentially tarnished her star—
some success in *The Bachelor and the Bobby Soxer,*
Fort Apache with handsome hubby Agar.

In 1950 she called it quits,
retiring from her glory days,
but worked as a U.S. ambassador
a role she had played in other ways.

In the Great Depression, spirits were low,
so Shirley brought escapism, smiles,
telling simple stories of love and loss
for the masses flocking the aisles.

For the Love of the Dance
"Can't sing. Can't act. Slightly balding. Can dance a little."
—casting agents about Fred Astaire.

Terpsichore did not bless me with her graceful gift,
and yet I had ambitions. Ballet lessons at five,
square dances in p.e. class, bluegrass clogging at a family reunion,
modern dance classes in college, keeping up with *Dance*
magazine and their love affairs with Graham, Nureyev,
Baryshnikov, Tharp, Fontaine, Farrell, Ailey,
Morris, Joffrey, Cunningham, Taylor, the Bolshoi,
all those leotards and tights stretched over taut bodies,
the polished wood of the studio floor, the ballet barre,
pliés reflected in wall-to-wall mirrors, mocking me.

Surrounding one's self with the illusion of dance
does not a dancer make. So, I worship from afar
Fosse jazz hands; Pilobolus' pretzels; Copeland's pas de deux;
and Fred Astaire movies, his tapping, sliding, prancing;
twirling Ginger, Jane, or Cyd, full skirts billowing,
long legs over their heads; top hat, cane, and white tails.

Loved *Singin' in the Rain* with Donald O'Connor,
Gene Kelley, and Debbie Reynolds hoofing it
on stage sets, tops of couches, mud puddles; *Seven Brides
for Seven Brothers*: All that log rolling, axe swinging,
jumping, and spinning!; Busby Berkeley extravaganzas
with dizzying kaleidoscopic dancers; or *White Christmas*
with Rosemary Clooney and Vera-Ellen with her teeny-tiny waist,
kicking up their heels with Bing and Danny
or any choreography of note—and since I'm no Pavlova
or Beyoncé, I'll contentedly watch *Thriller* zombies
line dance or Cagney tap "Yankee Doodle Dandy,"
my toe shoes, dried leather hanging on a peg.

Beatle Mania

The Beatles run, run, run
as fast as they can,
girls with beehives and cat-eyed glasses
in hot pursuit, just to touch the hem
of their suit coat or kiss their pointy boots
or stroke their skinny ties.
After all, it was a hard day's night.
Something must be done to assuage
the masses, so here they come
with their mop-tops and Liverpudlian charm,
Scouser accents, and sardonic wit
to the streets of London, knowing they can't
buy love and should have known better.
The birds want all their loving,
happy just to dance with this boy
or that boy as long as he is one of these boys.
The girls in the movie theater also scream and cry.
They forget about their Pepsis, yeah, yeah, yeah,
and their popcorn as soon as guitar chords fill the air.
They cry and cannot tell why the tears
drip down onto their Peter Pan collars
except it is some kind of pure power,
pure love that rocks the matinee,
rocks their world to its very core.

Ruminations

> "...what can she be/thinking of, striding into the ballroom/ where no black face has ever showed itself/except above a serving tray?" —"Hattie McDaniel Arrives at the Coconut Grove," Rita Dove

Lovely gardenias, so fragrant, so white,
along my arm, in my hair. It's a wonderful night!
Here I am, seated at a table by the kitchen.
Am I supposed to be grateful to the Ambassador
for bending their " policy": No Negroes Allowed? Ha!
Guess they think this *is* my place,
not a real actress. I paid my dues—
youngest of thirteen;
parents, former slaves;
washroom attendant, waitress, maid.
Hmmm, Vivian and Clark are up in front.
There's Selznick and Fleming. What glamour!
Linen-covered tables, delicate china cups.
All that gold on the dais.
Thinking back on my career, my music, singing,
acting—so many roles as maids!
Mammy—my people hate the stereotype,
the head rag, the voluminous apron,
but I held my own with Leigh, Gable, de Havilland.
The NAACP also hates it. 700.00 for playing
a maid is better than 7.00 for being one.
There's Fay Bainter on the podium, talking
"race, creed, and color." Now the award
for Best Supporting Actress.

Dear Lord, shine your light.

"Hattie McDaniel."

My name, my name!

"Hallelujah!"

They're standing, for me!

Seeking

"Resourceful, great Odysseus was happy,/ rejoicing in the land of his fathers." —The Odyssey, Homer

Dorothy Gale eventually gets it right
but initially sees the Kansas landscape
as nothing more than a boring farm
filled with horses, haystacks, and fields of corn
until a window sash cracks her on the head,
the family cow sails by the swirling house,
and Miss Gulch morphs into a cackling witch.
Her wish to go somewhere over the rainbow
is realized when technicolor flowers and little people appear;
she must flee the vengeful Witch of the West,
accompanied by the Scarecrow, the Tin Man, and the Cowardly Lion
to the Land of Oz where the Wizard gives them a dangerous task.
Dorothy has to learn her lesson
amidst the perils of angry apple trees, broomstick fires, sleep-inducing poppy fields,
flying monkeys, and castle incarceration.
When she sees her auntie's image in a crystal ball, she finally knows
her heart's desire.
After a perilous escape, a melted witch, and Toto's discovering
the fraudulent Wizard behind the curtain, Dorothy wants nothing
more than to go home, to her own *nostos*.
Of course, ethereal, giggling Glinda *could* have told her
the power to return was in those ruby slippers all along.
Nevertheless, she's back on the farm with Auntie Em and Uncle Henry,
de-tasseling corn, canning tomatoes, helping Zeke slop the hogs,
making the best of it, still singing about bluebirds, embroidering
her jeans with the Scarecrow's face.

That's Entertainment

In my time there were very few or no news reels
at the theater, certainly not montages of Panzers
or Hitler youth but ping-pong playing cats,
maybe a sequined starlet on Oscar night.
Mostly there were cartoons—
anthropomorphic animals like
Chilly Willy, Woody Woodpecker, Droopy,
Chip and Dale, Pepe Le Pew, Tom and Jerry,
Donald Duck, Goofy, Bugs Bunny, Pluto,
Porky Pig, Tweety Bird, Augie Doggie,
Daffy Duck, Huckleberry Hound,
Quick Draw McGraw, Sylvester the Cat,
Foghorn Leghorn, Andy Panda, Wile E. Coyote
Or lively characters like Little Lulu,
Popeye the Sailor, Elmer Fudd,
Yosemite Sam, Casper the Friendly Ghost,
certainly poetically alliterative, fun for everyone:
Twirling and whirling colors,
animated fights and flights,
boings and sproings and oiks and eeks,
skunky amour, anvils, carrot chomps,
hats, holes, tantrums, eyeballs,
and lots of love in the end.
These theatrical shorts came first
before any drama, history, or adventure
played out—later, Pixar caught the fever
with dancing desk lamps, tin toys, lava flows,
blue umbrellas, and baby pipers.
These little treats were sweet and melty,
like Raisinets or Goobers from paper boxes,
the *amuse bouche* before the main course.

Hepburn

Oh, Kate, you Yankee warbler, stick-thin scarecrow,
doe-eyed beauty, muscled athlete, screwball dame,
witty and wise, Shakespearean, closeted lover,
Tracy's gal pal, box office poison, lily lover,
riverboat virago, queen triumphant, old maid spinster,
you were my beautiful Jo, one-gloved like Michael Jackson,
wearing scorched gowns, climbing trees, putting on plays
with Meg, Amy, and Beth, chopping off your hair,
writing melodrama and heartfelt tales of the times,
your torrid love for little sister and Mr. Baer!
How I laughed at you singing to Baby,
a pet leopard, or playing with a paleontologist!
How I loved your pointy hats with sudden feathers
or folds of silken fabric, your pencil skirts, and stylish shoes!
There you were in the office, dictating copy, or on the links,
swinging a club, clearing the trees, Spencer by the tee.
Or Eleanor of Aquitaine, sparring with O'Toole,
your Henry. Or Mary Queen of Scots, riding into the highlands.
Or Tracy Lord, that stuck-up coquette,
sipping cocktails and kissing reporters on the sly.
Also, woman of the year, boiling black coffee,
adjusting a silk stocking or else a lawyer at odds with your husband,
a battle of the sexes over divorce and debate.
Here you are again in your dotage, hair pinned up,
wearing trousers, driving motorboats, listening to loons,
dancing solo in the shade of tall pines,
teaching us passion, joy.
I think of you in your nineties,
swimming in an ice-cold river, tasting a pot
of homemade soup, your hand atremble on the spoon,
and want to sit with you as twilight
touches your top-knot with streaks of darker gray,
watching the sun set from your Connecticut balcony.

Bedford Falls

Everyone wants to be missed when they're gone,
to have made a difference, to have been there
when needed, to have had George Bailey's
wonderful life. Yet, most of us never
saved our little brother from drowning
let alone a whole shipload of sailors.
Most of us never kept a whole community
safe from corruption, seediness, or squalor.
Our Granville house still needs a newel post,
replacement windows. Our neighbor died
from a poisonous overdose. The Building and Loan
continues to raise interest and overcharge
the middle class. More than likely
a suicidal man did drown in the river,
and Zuzu's petals never existed. The Potters
of the world seem to be winning
while all around the good guys
are still trying to lasso the moon.

Conflict

"It is well that war is so terrible, or else we might grow too fond of it." —Robert E. Lee

What does it say about us when we queue up
to see war movies—the guts and glory,
the blood and the bombs, rooting for the good guy,
sharing pathos within the theater
of war? The big screen amplifies the horror,
the heroism, though, in truth, our hearts
shrink and fibrillate in fear.
Still, I count myself as part of the effluence.

In a two-hour time frame, the exposition:
the set-up of innocents, patriots,
zealous generals, soldiers of every ilk;
the rising conflict among comrades
and enemies alike, fear, boredom,
escalation of terror;
a climactic battle or crucible;
the falling action: death, resignation,
a return to what can never
again be a sense of normalcy;
and the denouement: men and women
forever changed, shattered, saluting
a cold stone marker aflap with flags.

In real life, I am a pacifist,
penning poetry, peace and love,
a hippie, flowers in my hair.

We want war to stop,
no more maiming, missile launches, chemical
weapons, boots on the ground,
relegating such things
to mere action on a movie screen,
watching history, dead and buried.

Flight

Whatever happens to the little boy
in *Schindler's List*, the one who runs
and runs when his people are rounded up,
herded into showers raining Zyklon B,
shoved into ovens, burning night and day?
The boy, I mean, no bigger than a mouse,
eyes sunken and wide, searching for a hiding place.
The one shooed away by *kinder*
under floorboards so runs to the outhouse,
slips down the shithole
where other kids spattered with feces
sit shivering in the muck.
I'd like to think because of his intrepidity,
his constitution, he endures the stench,
the terror, and when darkness settles in,
he arises from the unholy font,
slinks around buildings, dodges searchlights,
shimmies beneath a loose bit of barbed wire,
tears his shirt, but bellies on until he is free
of the fence, once again, running and running,
into the looming woods, drinks from a stream,
washes his hands and face,
eats a handful of pale berries,
until someone kind, a hunter or a hiker,
comes upon him sleeping beneath a tree,
half-starved, britches stiff with shit,
and carries him like a baby to shelter,
gives him clean clothes, milk, bread, *leben*.

Visualization

Picture—a nail,
a little dirty.

No, a wooden spike.
Like the one driven through a vampire's heart.

Bela Lugosi at the drive-in.
Kids clad in pj's
in the back of a stationwagon
imitating the killing;
the speaker, a silver
spider clinging to daddy's window.

The spike,
hefted, rough
to the touch.

A mallet is required to ram it in,
to kill what is already dead.

Like betrayal, repeated.

Picture—a heart punctured,
black flow that should be red,
venous blood welling up
like lakes of darkness in duplicitous lives.

Parallels

Aunt Hazel didn't know that Hitchcock's *Marnie*
was a grown-up movie but took my young sister and me anyway,
the movie C rated, condemned by the Catholic Church.
Why, I wondered, does Marnie panic
at the sight of red gladiolas or red-coated riders
in a fox hunt? Why does she recoil at Sean Connery's touch,
James Bond, after all? We flinch when she shoots Forio, her beloved
    horse,
after he breaks his leg jumping a fence ("There, there now")
and are horrified to see the beautiful bride face-down
in a swimming pool the morning after Mark rips her negligee.
It all comes clear once Marnie remembers
late-night knocking on her mother Bernice's door,
sailors calling. Little Marnie has to wake up
and sleep on the couch to accommodate the clients.
Bruce Dern comes to her in a thunderstorm but roughs up the mother,
so her daughter—spoiler alert—kills him with a poker—blood, red—
("There, there now"). At movie's end, she drives away
with Mark, away from the past, sun breaking through the clouds.
Aunt Hazel herself never marries but gets engaged
to Woody, who, according to Hazel, afraid of sex,
perhaps a closeted homosexual, which Auntie whispers,
shoots himself two weeks before the wedding,
pan make-up smudging a singed hole in his temple,
pale and chaste in the tufted coffin.
We are never to talk about the movie nor about Woody
but still wonder about sex and violence, all around.

Fear and Loathing

The Puritan in me says, "Stay away, old Scratch!
You with your slitted red eyes, hooves, horns,
and scabrous skin!" In some tales, you are suave,
sophisticated, hiding beneath a fedora,
a red carnation in your lapel, but my nightmares
know better. It must have been the nuns
who described you so vividly, filling in,
with chalk, what sin does to your soul.
Every time I watch *Rosemary's Baby*
I am scared of the rape scene,
frail waifish Mia mauled and violated
by the venomous beast, all lust
and grunts, raking her marble skin
with pointy nails, naked chanters
all around; the eating of raw liver
and tainted mousse; tannis root
as a talisman, upside-down crosses,
but then there's Minnie, the nosy neighbor,
Ruth Gordon, a real hoot, that whine
of a woman, hair in curlers, a flamboyant
scarf, mixing chalky potions,
plucking Rosemary's knife
from her wooden floor,
providing comic relief from the fiendish
vision of the devil who climbed
out of hell and came to Manhattan
for a one-night stand in a stinking basement.

Ulysses as Porn

Credits roll: Leopold Bloom as leering loiterer
and Gerty MacDowell as lame flirt.
No whumpa-whumpa music here. Just *"Tantum Ergo"*
floating over Sandymount. Fireworks begin.
Leopold plays with his watch. Not in UPS shorts
but in mourner's black. She, not in mini skirt,
halter top, thong, but in blue, sporting a boater.
Litany of Mary is heard. Gerty shows garters,
sheer stockings. Rocket ascends.
Leopold leers, leans back on rock, hand in pocket.
Eyes meet. Legs widen. Over the strand
a Roman candle bursts into stars. Golden ones.
Oh, bright flashfleshfishflinchfun! Gerty licks
middle finger. Leopold licks lips.
Camera pulls back to long shot of Gert
limping towards Cissy. Tight shot on Leopold
who mouths, "Hot little devil."
Incense wafts from church window. Fade to black.

And the Winner is...
>"Not only is she cheap—but she's stupid." —Woody Allen
>about the character Linda Ash in Mighty Aphrodite

A retinue of women have won
    Oscars for playing prostitutes,
        nymphomaniacs, madams,
            drunkards, call girls, bad girls.

Anne Baxter as Sophie McDonald
    in *The Razor's Edge* turns
        to drink, debauchery after family
            perishes in a car crash.

Claire Trevor as Gaye Dawn
    in *Key Largo*, mistress, moll, lush,
        sings like a trained monkey,
            "Moanin' Low" for booze.

Donna Reed as Lorene, aka Alma,
    in *From Here to Eternity*, "hostess"
        of the New Congress Club,
            a hooker with a heart of gold.

Jo Van Fleet as Cathy Ames,
    aka Kate Trask in *East of Eden*,
        a money-grubbing Eve,
            a monstrous madam mother.

Dorothy Malone as Mary Lee Hadley,
    in *Written on the Wind*,
        daughter of an oil baron,
            nympho lusting after Rock.

Elizabeth Taylor as Gloria Wandrous
    in *Butterfield 8*, "slut of all time,"
        a hooker in a silky slip,
            a coat of mink.

Shirley Jones as Lulu Bains
    in *Elmer Gantry*, doxy
        seeking salvation
            and a preacher's love.

Jane Fonda as Bree Daniels,
    in *Klute*, pawn and prostitute,
        "best fuck in the world,"
            worth the price of a dishwasher.

Kim Basinger as Lynn Bracken
    in *L.A. Confidential*, Veronica
        Lake look-a-like, *femme fatale*
            with an eye for danger.

Mira Sorvino as porn star Linda Ash
    in *Mighty Aphrodite*, governed by fate,
        a Greek chorus and a director
            standing in judgment.

Consider Belle Watling, Sweet Charity,
    Irma, Lana, Shug, Ophelia, Vivian Ward.
        All, tainted, painted ladies,
            but no little men upon *their* mantels.

Bravo, brave actresses!
    You bring awareness,
        walking the red carpet,
            shrugging off any contiguous shame

of pock-marked pimps in back alleys,
    grooming runaways and naïfs,
        beating women with coat hangers,
            grabbing the gold every time,

or else you rise above
 the real-life casting couch,
  fighting off gropers and abusers
   shining in your own right.

Something

    Ordinary—
          coffee at home.

Out there—
      Superman goes by
          on a skateboard
              in a hoodie
                  letters on his jacket
                      mighty hieroglyphics.

Spiderman scales
      the high-rise wall—
          jelly hands.

There's a thin line between nothingness and heroics.

(I long for the heroic that is in you—
      a surprising climactic moment.)

Out there—
      Batman's signal lights
          the Gotham sky.

In here—
      dried bee in a window crack.

Songcatcher

I'd like to roam the mountains of North Carolina
wading in cold streams, warblers, veeries, and siskins
on the wing, fog awash on peaks,
the drama of Tanawha, sedges and spruce,
and collect tunes from folks who know
"Mary of the Wild Moor," "Moonshiner,"
and "Fair and Tender Ladies," crooned and warbled
on front porch chairs, salamanders askitter
in the goldenrod, silverlings dancing in the moonlight,
and all the cliff edges alive with avens.
My backpack filled with poetry,
I'd hike back down, push play, bake cornbread,
cook butter beans, sit a spell and rock back and forth,
back and forth, humming, eyes closed,
floating on reveries of misty blue.

In the Midst of Movies, Poetry

When Lee reads "somewhere i have never travelled gladly beyond"
with its line, "nobody, not even the rain, has such small hands,"
all the poets sigh, beating feet to the bookshelf,
inhaling cumming's poem like aromatherapy.

At Finch's funeral, Karen reads:
"And round that early-laurelled head
Will flock to gaze the strengthless dead,
And find unwithered on its curls
The garland briefer than a girl's,"
commemorating her lover, an intrepid pilot
dying, like the athlete, young.

John Keating bellows, "Oh, Captain, my Captain,"
"I sound my barbaric yawp," and *carpe diem*,
to scholar poets sad, rebellious, fragile,
wearing willow boughs and wings.

The photojournalist, Kurtz's lackey,
babbling and half mad, wishes to be "a pair
of ragged claws scuttling across floors of silent seas."
recalling angsty Prufrock, the etherized patient,
sea girls wreathed in red and brown, in a Cambodian
jungle, a place of beheadings, hangings,
the heart of darkness, the horror.

Such enriching lines surprise, serenade,
bringing us back to books and bards,
thrilling us even as we roll out of the dark
of the theater into the bright light
of the real world that so desperately
craves a poetic touch or such an interlude,
serendipitous, a swirled heart in our coffee.

Holding On

In "Ode on Intimations of Immortality," the American bard
sings of romping youth, joy in the glens and glades,
and as years slip by like swirling leaves in a stream,
consolation in remembrance, sumptuous flowers,
what youth brings, embracing the remains
though splendor in the grass is forever first gone.
Such is Deannie's recitation in the last scene
of Kazan's masterwork whose title evokes
the good gray wound-dresser who too would have loved
Bud stretching in jersey or wife beater, soft-lipped,
singing, unbridled, sensuous, while Deannie's
repressiveness chokes her like a rushing waterfall,
poor babbling Ophelia, floundering in the mad foam,
desire like an anchor pulling her below.

Ode to Haley Mills
"Listen! I have the most scaaaaathingly brilliant idea!"
—*The Trouble With Angels*

Most people think you were
just an old-maid schoolteacher
on "Saved by the Bell,"
but what they didn't know
is we knew you when,
wanted to *be* you,
to talk like you
with a British accent,
to act like you,
Pollyanna donning a straw hat,
posing and simpering
with that darn cat,
scaling baobab trees,
plummeting down cataracts,
a pigtailed castaway,
bamboozling Mother Superior,
attempting to save geeky Mary
from drowning in the pool,
smoking cigarettes in the convent,
setting fires in *The Chalk Garden*,
kissing a boy in Crete,
singing "Let's get together,"
a duet with yourself,
bandaging a wound,
putting a lizard on Brian Keith's girlfriend,
widening blue eyes,
mouth agape in amazement,
flipping blonde bangs,
sitting on white sand
with a perfectly puckered brow,
wondering about first love,
moonlight on the water,
future contracts with Disney.

What She Wore Oscar Night, 2001

She wore a swan for a dress,
no bell-beat of wings,
no brilliance upon lake,
a still head resting.

"I was going to wear my swan too—
but it was so last year," quips Martin.
2000 was not a good year for swans,
we think, pondering "I've Seen It All."

But Bjork lost to Dylan
for "Things Have Changed,"
sans swan, sans attendance,
dressed like a preacher man.

Beyond the city and the Shrine,
a lamentation of swans rises
into the plumage of sky, then rests in reeds
near scalloped shores.

The Gunderson Baby

Not long after Marge
finds the thugs, one
fleeing across a frozen lake,
one, in a wood chipper,
she and Norm settle in
for a time, five o'clock visits
to the buffet where they
overeat wild rice hot dish and Tater Tots,
final check-ups at the Ob/Gyn,
late night digs into a pickle jar,
more desk work than field assignments,
until the baby is finally born:
little Lars, all ten fingers and toes,
eleven pounds, three ounces
a compact bundle of joy.
Marge nurses Lars while
watching the Vikings or Packers,
Norm munching pretzels,
swilling Hamm's or Grain Belt.
Marge burps Lars
on her diaper-draped shoulder,
Norm, snoozing, salty crumbs on his shirt,
the snow falling outside
like the soft flakes of Narnia,
the sky perpetually white.

Sound Surround

Nothing we do is really quiet.
Even as I type this, the pick-pock-pick
of computer keys signals I am here.
Thinking is quiet but *something* synapses.
In *A Quiet Place*, the Abbots
ably shuffle barefooted on sand,
play with soft toys, sign their wants
and needs and can only speak beneath
the roar of a waterfall or a rushing
river. We know it cannot last—
the buzz and bing of a battery space shuttle,
the groans of childbirth, a scream of pain
arouse the giant-eared beings
who listen for the errant sounds
of creatures who can't be fully
silent, living in a world filled with crunch
and tap and roar and rattle,
the cries of humanity, heartbeats
pent up in a post-apocalyptic place.
The only real quiet is the quiet of death,
then and only then are you really safe.

Little Girl

In the photo, I am five years old.
I lie upon my father's chest,
heartbeat, steady, strong, comforting.

I fall asleep, listening.

In the movie, Hushpuppy holds a chick to her ear,
hearing its gristled heart.

A dead crow makes no sound,
glossy on the wet ground.

In the distance,
beastly aurochs, storm clouds
threaten life in the Bathtub.

Hushpuppy's father's heart slows down.

Slows   down.

Ceases.

Everybody loses the thing that made them.

grief

it's true	it does	come	in waves
like those	rolling	onshore	in *Manchester*
by the Sea	gray	cold	deep
symphonic	sadness	playing	o'er top
an empty pier	the clanking	of halyards	bobbing
boats	moored	in a wintry	marina
heavy	clouds	rain	sleet
rattling	planks	your heart	broken
welling	of tears	fears	sadness
ghost	that never	disappears	returns
arising	from nowhere	somewhere	in waves
threatening	to take you	below	drowning
engulfing	your life	so painful	so painful

Patsey

Patsey rolls toward Solomon,
her chemise thin like her,
craving a gentle touch
since she's used
like a horse in harness
to burden with sacks
of picked cotton,
500 pounds a day,
to whip and brutalize.
She's injured and raped
by a composite monster, mistress/
master, demons
in the dangerous night.
She, a pillar of strength,
an African queen
dressed up like a battered
doll for tea and cake
or in burlap or rags
fit for the field.
Though her back is scarred,
her eye full of blood,
she can stare down the sun.
Her anguish knows no end.

Acting the Part

Daniel Day Lewis's Lincoln
is a high talker, carrying Willy
upon his long back, top-hatted
on his horse amid the carnage
of Petersburg, refusing gloves
on his way to Ford's, lank and pale
upon the boarding-house bed,
belonging to the ages
at the end of it all.
How soon we forget
until historical drama
sweeps us along,
reminding us of heroes,
our humanity, mythologizing
no more as we remember
the difficult days of war,
the business of politics,
enslavement of a race.
"Now, now!" he declares
which echoes in our collective
conscience as we look
to the White House of our day,
hucksters and pettifoggers
abounding, reducing policy
to tweets and twits.
Oh, that a Lincoln would rise up
to speak eloquently against
a rising tide of fear and chicanery,
high talking us down
to earth, to walk boldly again
beneath the murky night!

Notes and Movie Allusion Titles

—Persistence of vision refers to the optical illusion that occurs when visual perception of an object does not cease for some time after the rays of light proceeding from it have ceased to enter the eye, thus, animation/the art of film is born. (*Wikipedia.com*)
—page 1: Eadweard Muybridge was an English photographer, a pioneer in photographic studies of motion, and early work in motion-picture projection. Leland Stanford was an industrialist and horseman interested in gait analysis, owner of the horse Sallie Gardner, a first animated subject
—page 2: Charlie Chaplin, the Little Tramp, was an important British silent screen star, comic, filmmaker. *Modern Times*
—page 7: *A Hard Day's Night*
—page 8: Actress Hattie McDaniel won Best Supporting Actress for her role as Mammy in *Gone With the Wind* (1939), the first African-American actor to win an Oscar
—page 10: *The Wizard of Oz*
—page 12: *The African Queen, Little Women, Bringing Up Baby, Desk Set, Pat and Mike, The Lion in Winter, Mary of Scotland, The Philadelphia Story, Woman of the Year, Adam's Rib,* and *On Golden Pond*
—page 13: *It's a Wonderful Life*
—page 16: *The Vampire*
—page 19: allusion to the novel *Ulysses* by James Joyce
—page 24: *Songcatcher*
—page 25: *Hannah and Her Sisters; Out of Africa; The Dead Poets' Society;* and *Apocalypse Now*
—page 26: *Splendor in the Grass*; the American bard and the "good gray wound-dresser" is Walt Whitman who served as a nurse in the Civil War
—page 27: *Pollyanna, That Darn Car, The Castaways, The Trouble With Angels, The Parent Trap,* and *The Moonspinners*
—page 28: At the 2001 Oscars, singer Bjork wore a dress shaped like a dead swan; her song "I've Seen It All" (from *Dancer in the Dark*) lost for Best Original Song to Bob Dylan's "Things Have Changed" (from *Wonder Boys*)

—page 29: *Fargo*
—page 31: *Beasts of the Southern Wild*
—page 33 *12 Years a Slave*
—page 34: *Lincoln*

www.ingramcontent.com/pod-product-compliance
Lightning Source LLC
LaVergne TN
LVHW050045090426
835510LV00043B/3202